SAM SMITH
IN THE LONELY HOUR

ISBN 978-1-4950-0083-6

HAL•LEONARD®
CORPORATION

7777 W. BLUEMOUND RD. P.O. BOX 13819 MILWAUKEE, WI 53213

Visit Hal Leonard Online at
www.halleonard.com

MONEY ON MY MIND

Words and Music by SAM SMITH
and BENJAMIN ROSS ASH

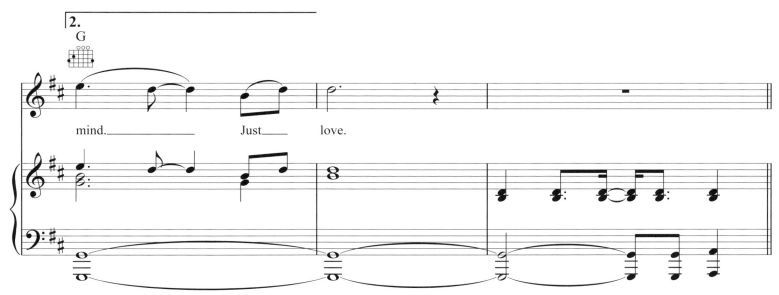

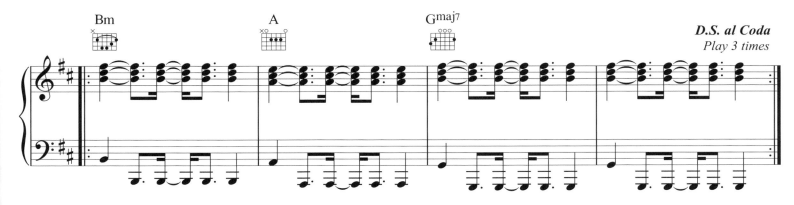

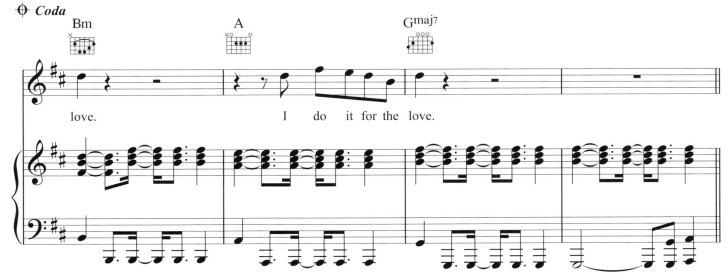

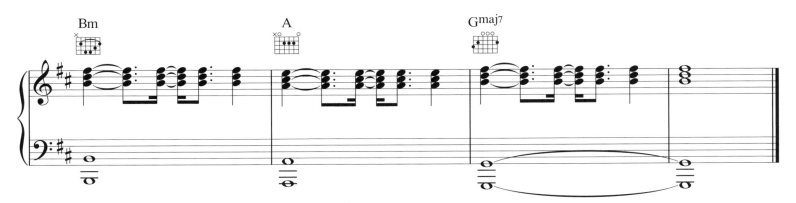

GOOD THING

Words and Music by SAM SMITH
and EG WHITE

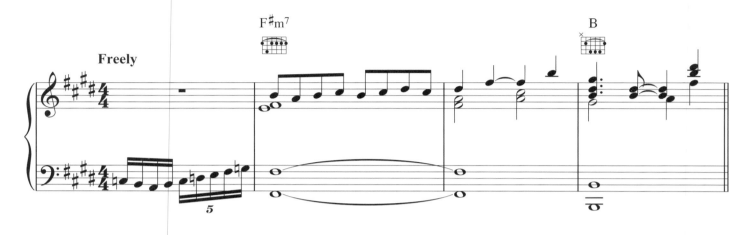

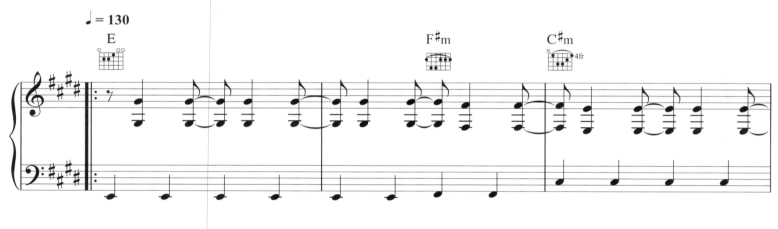

1. I had a dream__ I was mugged out-side your
2. We__ talk__ may-be twen-ty times a

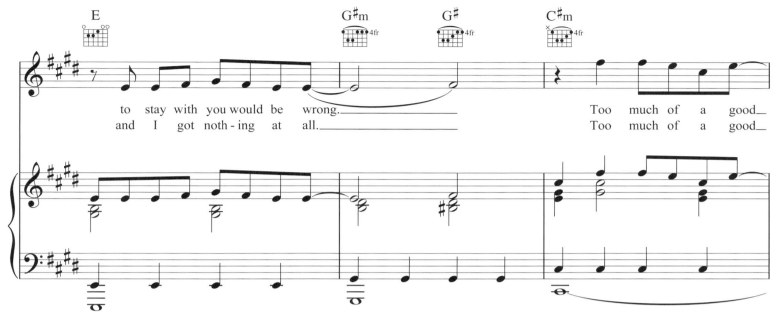

to stay with you would be wrong._____
and I got noth-ing at all._____

Too much of a good__
Too much of a good__

___ thing,___
___ thing,___

won't be good an-y-more.___
is-n't good and you know.___

To Coda ⊕ | 1.

Watch where I tread___ be-fore_ I___ fall.
I watch where I walk___ be-fore_ I___ fall,_

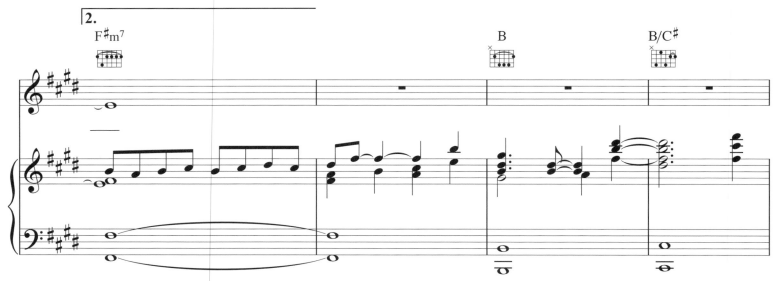

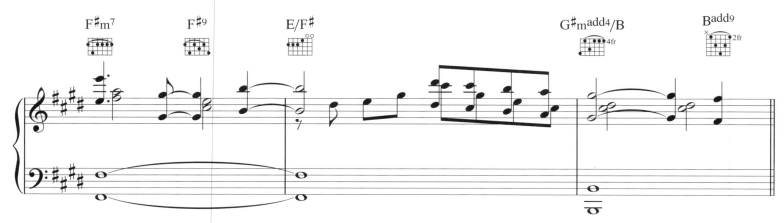

D.S. al Coda

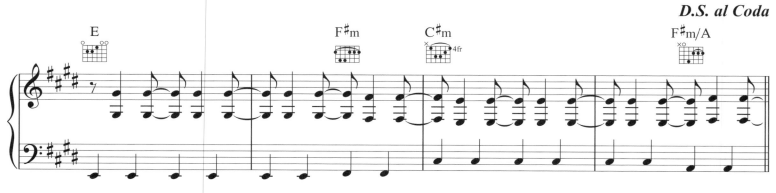

$\oplus$ *Coda*

be - fore I fall.

STAY WITH ME

Words and Music by SAM SMITH,
JAMES NAPIER and WILLIAM EDWARD PHILLIPS

1. Guess it's true I'm not good at a one night stand.
2. Why am I so e - mo - tion - al?

But I still need love 'cause I'm just a man.___
No, it's not a good look, gain some self con - trol.___

LEAVE YOUR LOVER

Words and Music by SAM SMITH
and SIMON ALDRED

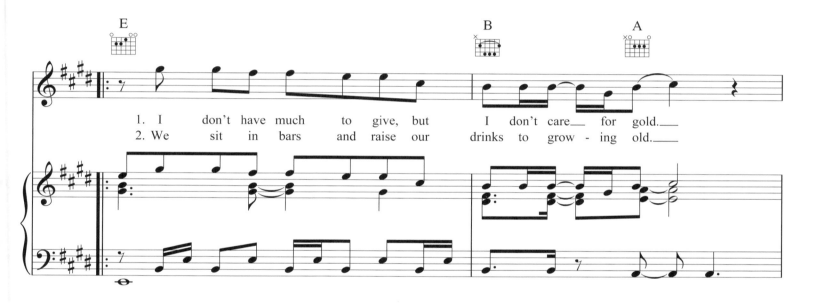

1. I don't have much to give, but I don't care__ for gold.__
2. We sit in bars and raise our drinks to grow-ing old.__

What use is mon-ey, when you need some-one__ to hold?__
Oh, I'm in love with you and you will nev-er know.__

Leave your___ lo - ver,___ leave him for me.___

leave him for me.___ Leave your___ lo - ver,___ leave him for me.___

I'M NOT THE ONLY ONE

Words and Music by SAM SMITH
and JAMES NAPIER

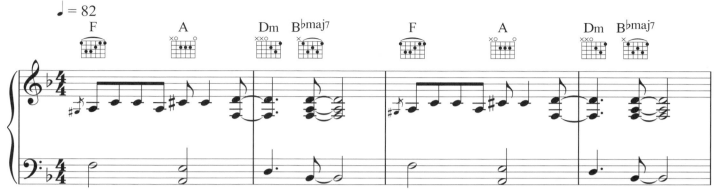

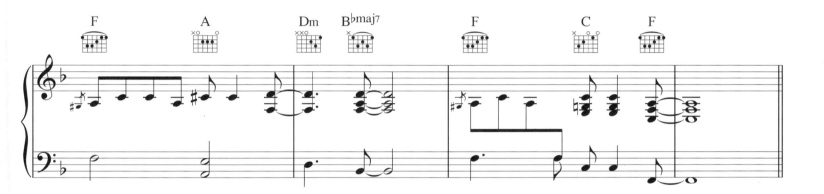

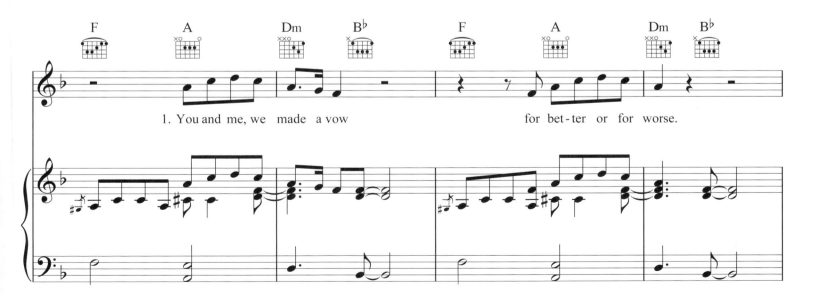

1. You and me, we made a vow   for bet-ter or for worse.

I'VE TOLD YOU NOW

Words and Music by SAM SMITH
and EG WHITE

1. You know what I mean. It's like walk-ing in the heat all day___ with no wa - ter.___
2. You know what I mean. Al - though___ I___ try my best I still let down the team.___

It's like wait-ing for a friend watch-ing ev-'ry-bod-y else meet theirs___ on that
You're ev -'ry-thing I want. Why should I___ re - sist when you are there for

LIKE I CAN

Words and Music by SAM SMITH
and MATT PRIME

stran - ger____ you gave a se - cond glance. He could be a
(3.)-coun - ter____ of____ cir - cum - stance. May - be, he's a

tro - phy____ of a one night stand. He could have your hu - mour____ but I
man - tra____ keeps your mind en - tranced. He could be the si - lence____ in this

don't un - der - stand____ 'cause he'll nev-er love you like I can, can, can.
may - hem,__ but then a - gain,

LIFE SUPPORT

Words and Music by SAM SMITH
and BENJAMIN ROSS ASH

1. I've been sleep-ing with the lights_ on 'cause the dark-ness is sur-round-ing you.
2. Sick of wak-ing up in dark - ness when the sky is al-ways paint - ed blue.

*top line 2º only till **

This is my world, this is my__ choice and you're the drug that gets me through.
There's a meth-od to my mad - ness. It's clear that you don't have a clue.

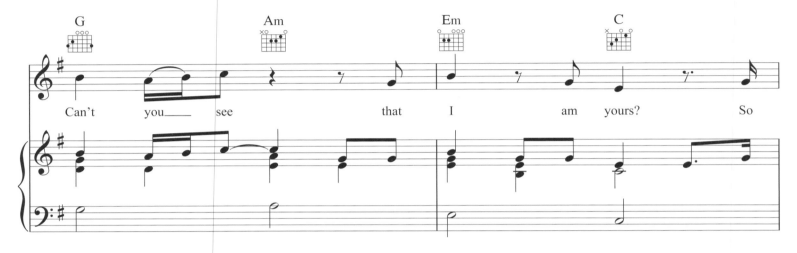

Can't you___ see that I am yours? So

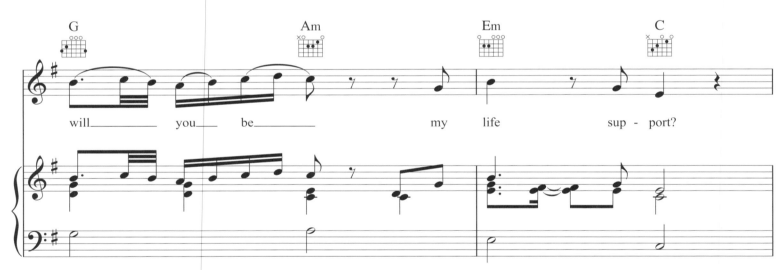

will___ you___ be___ my life sup - port?

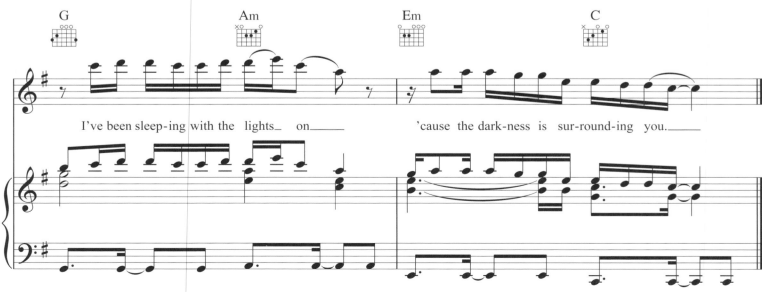

I've been sleep-ing with the lights_ on___ 'cause the dark-ness is sur-round-ing you.___

NOT IN THAT WAY

Words and Music by SAM SMITH
and FRASER T. SMITH

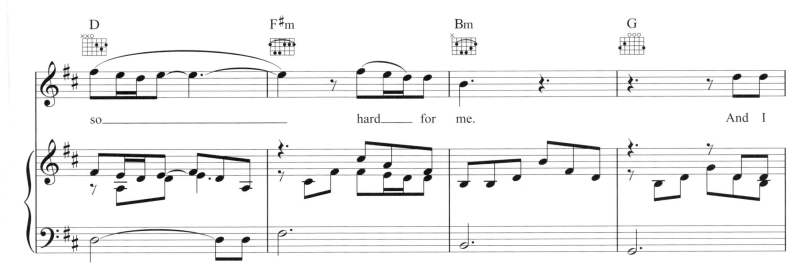

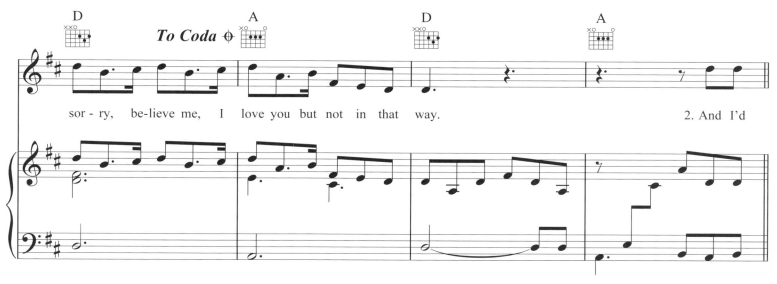

To Coda

D · A · D · A

sor - ry, be-lieve me, I love you but not in that way.　　　　2. And I'd

D · F#m · Bm · G

hate_____ to say___ I need you,_____ I'm so re-

D · F#m · Bm · G

-li - ant. I'm so de - pen - dent. I'm such a fool._____

LAY ME DOWN

Words and Music by SAM SMITH,
JAMES NAPIER and ELVIN SMITH

Poco rubato (♩ = 50)

Emaj7

Yes, I do, I be-lieve. That one day I will be where I was right there, right next to you.___

Aadd9

___ And it's hard, the days just seem so dark. The moon, the stars are noth-ing with-out you. Your

Emaj7

touch, your skin, where do I be-gin? No words can ex-plain the way I'm miss-ing you.___

make sure you're al - right._____ I'll take care of you,_____ I

don't want to be here if I can't be with you__ to - night._____ I'm

Soft 16th swing (♩ = 60)

reach-ing out to you,_____ can you hear__ my__ call?_____ (Who's to say you won't

hear me?)__ This hurt that I've been through._____ I'm miss-ing you, miss-ing you like

cra - zy,____ oh._____ You

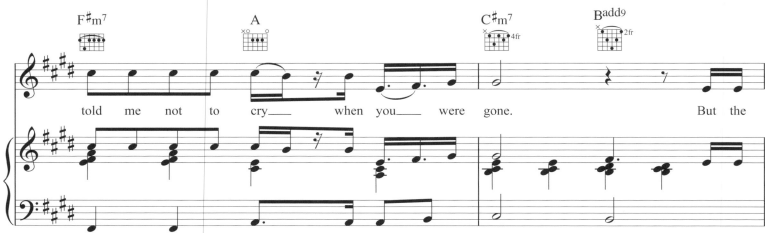

told me not to cry____ when you____ were gone. But the

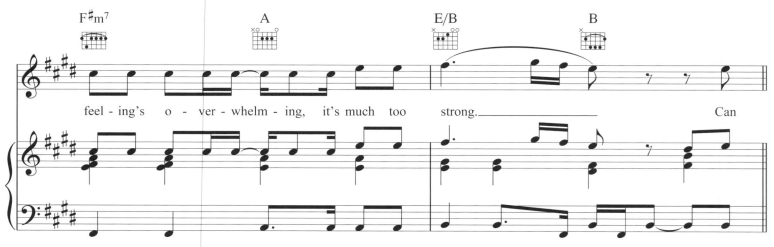

feel - ing's o - ver - whelm - ing, it's much too strong.____ Can

I lay by your____ side?_____ Next to

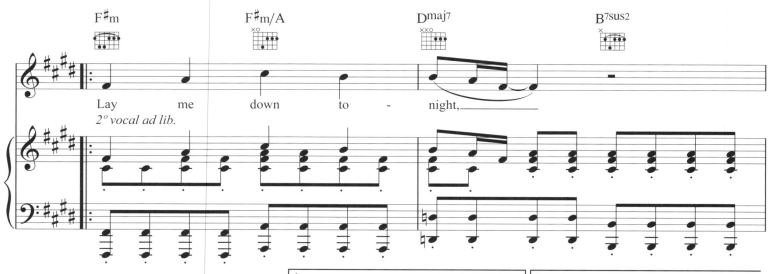

Lay me down to - night,_____

2° vocal ad lib.

lay me by your side._____

1.

side._____

2.

side._____ Can

Poco rubato (♩ = 50)

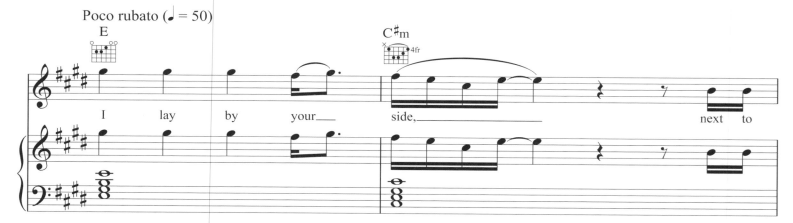

I lay by your___ side,_____ next to

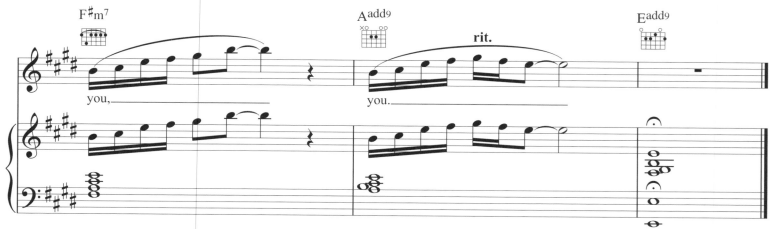

you,_____ you._____

rit.

RESTART

Words and Music by SAM SMITH
and ZANE LOWE

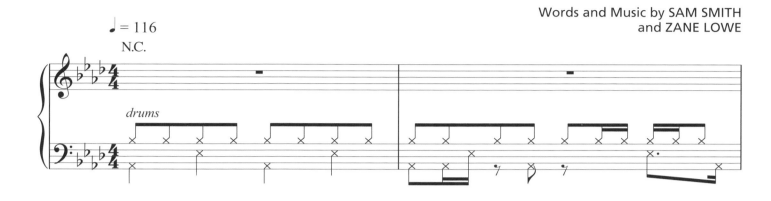

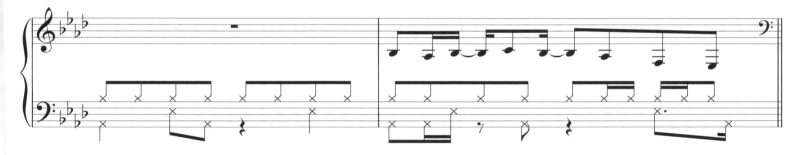

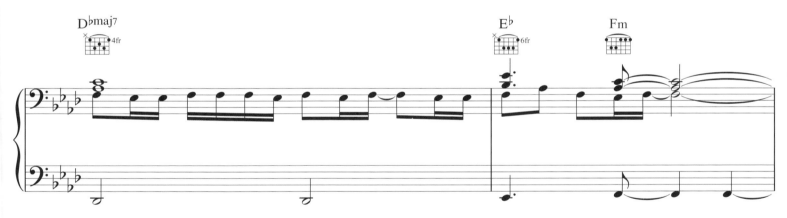

LATCH

Words and Music by GUY LAWRENCE,
HOWARD LAWRENCE, JAMES NAPIER
and SAM SMITH

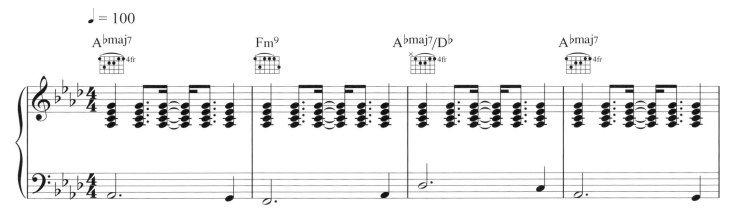

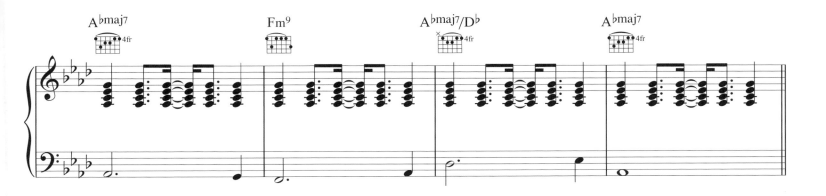

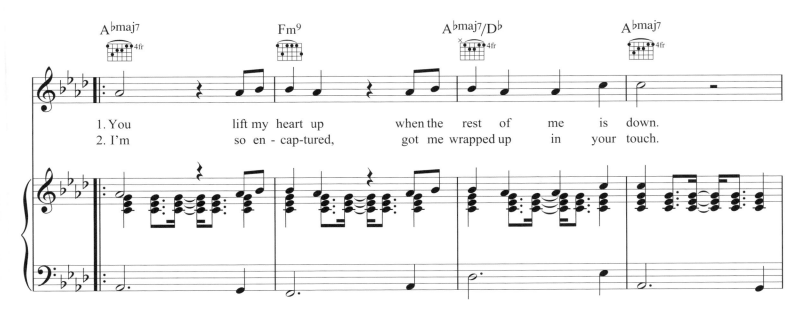

1. You lift my heart up when the rest of me is down.
2. I'm so en-cap-tured, got me wrapped up in your touch.

LA LA LA

Words and Music by AL HAKAM EL KAUBAISY,
JAMES MURRAY, MUSTAFA OMER,
SAM SMITH, SHAHID KHAN,
JAMES NAPIER, JONNIE COFFER
and FROBISHER MBABAZI

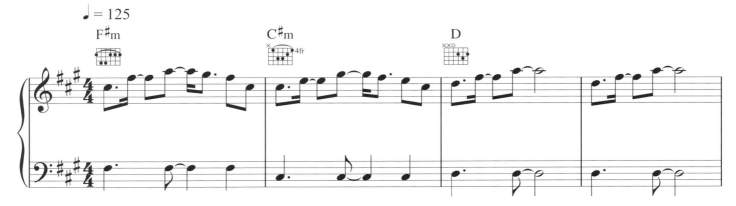

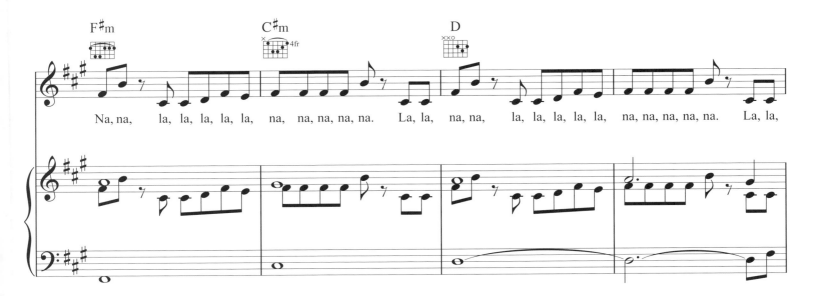

Na, na, la, la, la, la, la, na, na, na, na, na. La, la, na, na, la, la, la, la, la, na, na, na, na, na. La, la,

MAKE IT TO ME

Words and Music by SAM SMITH,
JAMES NAPIER and HOWARD LAWRENCE